FOR EDUCATIONAL

AND ENTERTAINMENT

PURPOSES ONLY

TRAVELERS

SOVEREIGN'S GUIDE FOR TRAVELING IN HONOR

Sovereign Publishing
TRAVELERS: SOVEREIGN'S GUIDE FOR TRAVELING IN HONOR

ISBN: 978-1-7337968-2-8

First Edition 2023
by Sovereign Publishing

Printed in the United States of America

WELCOME

While the contents of this guide is not exhaustive, may it serve you well in your efforts to self-govern in honor. May the Lord protect and bless you and your family, from bumper to bumper, while traveling throughout this land, and may everything you set your hands to and every place you venture, be blessed. Deuteronomy 28:6-8

In His Redeeming Grip,

dm

SOVEREIGN BEINGS

editor's opinion

Sovereigns believe one does not transfer complete trust, authority, or power to another person, group, or government. Instead, they always retain the ability to self-govern while seeking to protect and honor others at all times. Sovereigns are free people who retain their God-given rights protected by the Constitution for the United States of America.

"Men must be governed by God or they will be governed by Tyrants" - William Penn

The United States of America is a unique nation. It was the first constitutional republic formed in the world. Before the American Revolution, the King of England owned all the land in his colonies and the inhabitants of the colonies were his subjects. When the war was over, the King signed a Treaty of Paris, in 1783. This peace treaty transferred ownership over all the land in his colonies to the people. The King then relinquished all his sovereign powers, NOT to the government of the colonies, but to — the People, thereby making all the people of the land sovereign. This has never happened before or since in any other country.

Unlike other countries, where only the government is sovereign, in the United States, the People were declared sovereign and endowed by their Creator with rights. The government was then formed and instituted to serve its people, by securing their rights and freedoms. But with freedom comes responsibility. Unfortunately, America fell asleep on their watch, and that slumber created a hollowness in which a de facto assumption of power, whether by lawful authority or not, filled the void. Consequently, our rights and freedoms slowly faded into the background, giving way to the overbearing rise of all types of licenses, registrations, taxes, mandates, contracts, and statutes in exchange for a few privileges, like social security, Medicare, food stamps, government subsidies and the like.

Sovereign beings were never meant to be overburdened under the weightiness of an overreaching government democracy! Our government was created by sovereign people FOR the American people!

"WHENEVER PEOPLE ARE WELL-INFORMED THEY CAN BE TRUSTED WITH THEIR OWN GOVERNMENT" - THOMAS JEFFERSON -

CONTENTS

nt develops in
law
refer to a pa

SMITHS
30
30
AMPS
OIL
50
100
Morgan
WATER
FUEL
H
N

SOVEREIGN'S GUIDE

My people are destroyed for lack of knowledge. Hosea 4:6

While this guide may be invaluable to you as a compilation of many legal documents, it should NOT be considered legal advice. DO NOT accept this information, without first scrutinizing and understanding this information for yourself. I encourage you, as a Sovereign, to be skeptical before accepting any of these documents. That is why you will find a website link at the bottom of most pages, for further verification or research.

For decades, Americans have believed a state-issued driver's license is required to drive on all public streets and highways. After all, driver's education courses (once taught for free) have become every teen's sacred ceremonial "right of passage" into adulthood wherein one must first pass a state-approved driver's course, followed by a DMV driver's test. What if this was not intended?

The lawful TRUTH is, one's "right of passage", isn't a state issued driver's license or registration for their right to travel freely! This has been substantiated by numerous U.S. Court decisions, who confirm driving or traveling in one's own property is a Sovereign right and not a government-granted privilege.

What's the intended purpose of a driver's license? It was created by the Department of Transportation for those engaged in commerce, and "driving" their motor vehicle for hire and/or compensation. Examples include Uber drivers, limousine drivers, bus drivers, cab drivers, cargo drivers, and truck drivers.

But if your automobile was purchased for your private use, not commerce, it's your property to lawfully travel between points a and b, a purpose for which a license or registration was NEVER required.

Legislators, police officers, and court officials are quickly becoming aware of the many court decisions that continue to disprove the belief that driving is a privilege and therefore requires government approval, i.e. a license.

Examples like Thompson vs Smith 154 SE 579, which concluded "The right of the citizen to travel upon the public highways and to transport his property thereon, either by carriage or by automobile, is not a mere privilege which a city may prohibit or permit at will, but a common right which he has under the right to life, liberty, and the pursuit of happiness."

Statements like this are conclusive — the right to travel, without approval or restriction, is protected by the U.S. Constitution. There are numerous court decisions that communicate the same.

Many have to come to believe this is why it's valuable to fully comprehend the legal and lawful differences between traveling in private versus driving in commerce.

It might be valuable to know, while all licensed and registered commerce drivers are bound by government-enforced speed limits and traffic laws, Sovereigns are not looking for lawlessness permission while asserting their right to travel in private. On the contrary, with a culture of honor mindset, they feel duty bound to the Creator to honor the rules of the road. This motivates them to protect others at all costs.

In conclusion, even if you currently have a driver's license with a registration tag on your car, unless you are "driving in commerce", your rights are protected by law to "travel" freely without hindrance. It's your duty , however, to self-govern by staying safe on the roads and keeping others safe around you.

- Thomas Jefferson -

"Whenever people are well-informed they can be trusted with their own government".

GLOVE COMPARTMENT

MUST HAVES

FIFTH AMENDMENT RIGHTS

The Fifth Amendment creates a number of rights relevant to both criminal and civil legal proceedings.

In criminal cases, the Fifth Amendment guarantees the right to a grand jury, forbids "double jeopardy," and protects against self-incrimination.

It also requires that "due process of law" be part of any proceeding that denies a citizen "life, liberty or property" and requires the government to compensate citizens when it takes private property for public use.

AMENDMENT V

No person shall be held to answer for a capital, or otherwise, infamous crime, unless on a presentment or indictment of a grand jury, except in cases arising in the land or naval forces, or in the militia, when in actual service in time of war or public danger; nor shall any person be subject for the same offense to be twice put in jeopardy of life or limb; nor shall be compelled in any criminal case to be a witness against himself, nor be deprived of life, liberty, or property, without due process of law; nor shall private property be taken for public use, without just compensation.

Fifth Amendment protects against self-incrimination.

SELF-GOVERNING QUESTIONS?

Does the Fifth Amendment protect against self-incrimination? How might this be valuable to you? Will respectfully remaining silent, signal that you know your rights? Would the response, "I don't answer questions" be considered dismissive or dishonoring?

https://constitution.congress.gov/constitution/amendment-5/#amendment-5
www.law.cornell.edu/wex/fifth_amendment

"UCC 1-308"

PERFORMANCE OR ACCEPTANCE UNDER RESERVATION OF RIGHTS.

(a) A party that with explicit reservation of rights performs or promises performance or assets to performance in a manner demanded or offered by the other party does not thereby prejudice the rights reserved. Such words as "without prejudice," "under protest," or the like are sufficient.

"UNDER DURESS UCC 1-308"

In law, "under duress" refers to a situation where someone is forced, coerced, or threatened to do something against the person's will.

In other words, when a person is forced to do something under duress, it means that the person would not have normally acted or behaved that way.

The word "duress" is defined by the Merriam-Webster Dictionary as "forcible restraint or restriction" or "compulsion by threat".

So when you are under duress, it means that you are under pressure to do something or you are threatened to do something.

"WITHOUT PREJUDICE UCC 1-308"

When you use this, you are saying, "I reserve my right not to be compelled to perform under any contract or commercial agreement that I did not enter knowingly, voluntarily, and intentionally. I do not accept the liability of the compelled benefit of any unrevealed contract or commercial agreement."

SELF-GOVERNING QUESTIONS?

If you are nervous about your required signature on any document, would writing this code in its place, "UCC1-308", "Under Duress UCC1-308" or "Without Prejudice UCC1-308" be valuable?

www.law.cornell.edu/ucc/1/1-308

TEXAS TRANSPORTATION CODE

SECTION 521.001 - DRIVER'S LICENSE

(3). "DRIVER'S LICENSE" means an authorization issued by the department for the operation of A MOTOR VEHICLE.

The term includes:

(A) a temporary license or learner license; and

(B) an occupational license.

SELF-GOVERNING QUESTIONS?

According to the transportation code, to occupationally drive a motor vehicle, is a driver's license required while operating in commerce?

TEXAS TRANSPORTATION CODE

SECTION 201.904 - SPEED SIGNS

The department shall erect and maintain on the highways and roads of this state appropriate signs that show the maximum lawful speed for commercial motor vehicles, truck tractors, truck trailers, truck semitrailers, and motor vehicles engaged in the business of transporting passengers for compensation or hire (buses).

LAWFUL SPEED FOR :

- commercial motor vehicles,
- truck tractors,
- truck trailers,
- truck semitrailers,
- and motor vehicles engaged in the business of transporting passengers for compensation or hire (buses)

Acts 1995, 74th Leg., ch. 165, Sec. 1, eff. Sept. 1, 1995.

SELF-GOVERNING QUESTIONS?

According to the transportation code, are speeding signs required to alert commercial motor vehicles, like truck tractors, truck trailers, truck semitrailers, and motor vehicles engaged in business for hire? Does this transportation code address private non-commercial travelers?

https://texas.public.law/statutes/tex._transp._code_section_201.904

TEXAS TRANSPORTATION CODE

SECTION 502.003 - REGISTRATION

(a) Except as provided by Subsection (b), a political subdivision of this state

MAY NOT require an owner of a motor vehicle to:

(1) register the vehicle;
(2) pay a motor vehicle registration fee; or
(3) pay an occupation tax or license fee in connection with a motor vehicle.

b) This section does not affect the authority of a municipality to:

(1) license and regulate the use of motor vehicles for compensation within the municipal limits; and

(2) impose a permit fee or street rental charge for the operation of each motor vehicle used to transport passengers for compensation, other than a motor vehicle operating under a registration certificate from the department or a permit from the federal Surface Transportation Board.

(c) A fee or charge under Subsection (b) may not exceed two percent of the annual gross receipts from the vehicle.

(d) This section does not impair the payment provisions of an agreement or franchise between a municipality and the owners or operators of motor vehicles used to transport passengers for compensation.

Acts 1995, 74th Leg., ch. 165, Sec. 1, eff. Sept. 1, 1995. Amended by Acts 1997, 75th Leg., ch. 165, Sec. 30.45, eff. Sept. 1, 1997.

SELF-GOVERNING QUESTIONS?

Do you need a driver's license or registration to travel freely and privately in your automobile? Are non-commercial Travelers with integrity, duty-bound to keep others safe on the road safe and if anyone is harmed, are there consequences?

https://texas.public.law/statutes/tex._transp._code_section_502.003

TEXAS TRANSPORTATION CODE

SEC. 546.002 - LEGAL USE OF VISUAL (FLASHING) LIGHTS

Sec. 546.002

(a) "police escort" means facilitating the movement of a funeral, oversized or hazardous load, or other traffic disruptions for public safety purposes by a peace officer

(b) Sec. 546.001 (Permissible Conduct)(2), (3), and (4) apply only when the operator is:
(1) responding to an emergency call;
(2) pursuing an actual or suspected violator of the law;
(3) responding to but not returning from a fire alarm;
(4) directing or diverting traffic for public safety purposes; or
(5) conducting a police escort.

SELF-GOVERNING QUESTIONS?

According to this code, if you are traveling in private and no violation of the law has been committed, ie. bank robbery, hit and run, murder suspect, etc, are flashing lights considered a legal way to pull you over? If you do not feel safe on a dark road late at night, is it ok to call a 911 operator to assist you versus having to pull over alone in the middle of no where?

https://texas.public.law/statutes/tex._transp._code_section_546.002

SEC. 546.004 - LEGAL USE OF VISUAL (FLASHING) LIGHTS

546.004 EXCEPTIONS TO SIGNAL REQUIREMENT.

(c) A police officer may operate an authorized emergency vehicle for a law enforcement purpose, WITHOUT using the audible or visual signals required by

Section 546.003 if the officer is:

(1) responding to an emergency call or
(2) pursuing a suspected violator of the law with probable cause to believe that;
(3) responding to but not returning from a fire alarm;
(4) directing or diverting traffic for public safety purposes; or
(5) conducting a police escort.

Section 546.003 if the officer is:

(1) responding to an emergency call or pursuing a suspected violator of the law with probable cause to believe that:

(A) knowledge of the presence of the officer will cause the suspect to:
(i) destroy or lose evidence of a suspected felony;
(ii) end a suspected continuing felony before the officer has obtained sufficient evidence to establish grounds for arrest; or
(iii) evade apprehension or identification of the suspect or the suspect's vehicle; or
(B) because of traffic conditions on a multi-laned roadway, vehicles moving in response to the audible or visual signals may:
(i) increase the potential for a collision; or
(ii) unreasonably extend the duration of the pursuit; or
(2) complying with a written regulation relating to the use of audible or visible signals adopted by the local government that employs the officer or by the department.

TEXAS TRANSPORTATION CODE

SEC. 701.001-.002 - ARE THEY A TRAFFIC OFFICER

TEXAS TRANSPORTATION CODE Sec. 701.001. AUTHORIZATION

(a) Except as provided by Subsection (c), acting in conjunction with the sheriff of the county, the commissioner's court of a county may employ NOT MORE THAN FIVE REGULAR DEPUTIES AS COUNTY TRAFFIC OFFICERS.

(b) Except as provided by Subsection (c), the commissioner's court may employ not more than two additional deputies as county traffic officers to aid the regular officers in special emergencies.

(c) The limitation on the number of deputies that may be employed under Subsections (a) and (b) does not apply to a county with a population of more than two million.

TEXAS TRANSPORTATION CODE Sec. 701.002. POWER TO ACT; GUIDANCE

(a) A county traffic officer:
   (1) must be deputized by the sheriff or a constable of the county in which the officer is employed;
   (2) must give a bond and take an oath of office as other deputy sheriffs;
   (3) must work under the direction of the sheriff; and
   (4) has the same right and duty as a deputy sheriff to arrest a person who violates a law.

(b) Repealed by Acts 2009, 81st Leg., R.S., Ch. 471, Sec. 2, eff. June 19, 2009.

SELF-GOVERNING QUESTIONS?

What type of Traffic Officer can enforce commerce traffic violations and a county may not employ more than 5 deputies as traffic officers.?

https://statutes.capitol.texas.gov/Docs/TN/htm/TN.701.htm

SEC. 701.003 - ARE THEY A TRAFFIC OFFICER

TEXAS TRANSPORTATION CODE Sec. 701.003. DUTIES

(a) A county traffic officer shall:
   (1) be a motorcycle rider when practicable;
   (2) cooperate with the police department of each municipality in the county to enforce state traffic laws in that municipality and in the county;
   (3) enforce state laws that regulate the operation of a motor vehicle on a highway, street, or alley; and
   (4) remain on and patrol the highway at all times when performing the officer's duties.

(b) An officer may leave a highway only in pursuit of an offender the officer is unable to apprehend on the highway.

SELF-GOVERNING QUESTIONS?

What type of *official* has the *lawful protection* to perform the traffic stop of a *motor vehicle, whose operating in commerce*? Where do the state laws permit the regulating of a motor vehicle? When should a *county traffic officer* leave the highway?

18 U.S. CODE 241

CONSPIRACY AGAINST RIGHTS

If (TWO) or more persons conspire to injure, oppress, threaten, or intimidate any person in any State, Territory, Commonwealth, Possession, or District in the free exercise or enjoyment of any right or privilege secured to him by the Constitution or laws of the United States, or because of his having so exercised the same; or

If (TWO) or more persons go in disguise on the highway, or on the premises of another, with intent to prevent or hinder his free exercise or enjoyment of any right or privilege so secured—

They shall be fined under this title or imprisoned not more than ten years, or both; and if death results from the acts committed in violation of this section or if such acts include kidnapping or an attempt to kidnap, aggravated sexual abuse or an attempt to commit aggravated sexual abuse, or an attempt to kill, they shall be fined under this title or imprisoned for any term of years or for life, or both, or may be sentenced to death.

SELF-GOVERNING QUESTIONS?

Does the Constitution lawfully permit two or more officers to disguise themselves on the highway; or to injure, oppress, threaten, or intimidate the rights or privileges of another?

https://www.law.cornell.edu/uscode/text/18/241

18 U.S. CODE 242

DEPRIVATION OF RIGHTS UNDER COLOR OF LAW

Summary: it is a crime for a person acting under color of any law to willfully deprive a person of a right or privilege protected by the Constitution or laws of the United States.

For the purpose of Section 242, acts under "color of law" include acts not only done by federal, state, or local officials within their lawful authority, but also acts done beyond the bounds of that official's lawful authority, if the acts are done while the official is purporting to or pretending to act in the performance of his/her official duties. Persons acting under color of law within the meaning of this statute include police officers, prisons guards and other law enforcement officials, as well as judges, care providers in public health facilities, and others who are acting as public officials. It is not necessary that the crime be motivated by animus toward the race, color, religion, sex, handicap, familial status or national origin of the victim.

The offense is punishable by a range of imprisonment up to a life term, or the death penalty, depending upon the circumstances of the crime, and the resulting injury, if any.

Whoever, under color of any law, statute, ordinance, regulation, or custom, willfully subjects any person in any State, Territory, Commonwealth, Possession, or District to the "deprivation of any rights", privileges, or immunities secured or protected by the Constitution or laws of the United States, or to different punishments, pains, or penalties, on account of such person being an alien, or by reason of his color, or race, than are prescribed for the punishment of citizens, shall be fined under this title or imprisoned not more than one year, or both; and if bodily injury results from the acts committed in violation of this section or if such acts include the use, attempted use, or threatened use of a dangerous weapon, explosives, or fire, shall be fined under this title or imprisoned not more than ten years, or both; and if death results from the acts committed in violation of this section or if such acts include kidnapping or an attempt to kidnap, aggravated sexual abuse, or an attempt to commit aggravated sexual abuse, or an attempt to kill, shall be fined under this title, or imprisoned for any term of years or for life, or both, or may be sentenced to death.

SELF-GOVERNING QUESTIONS?

Would an official, WHOSE NOT a deputized county traffic officer, be seen as acting? What is the punishment for somone pretending to be a public official?

https://www.justice.gov/crt/deprivation-rights-under-color-law

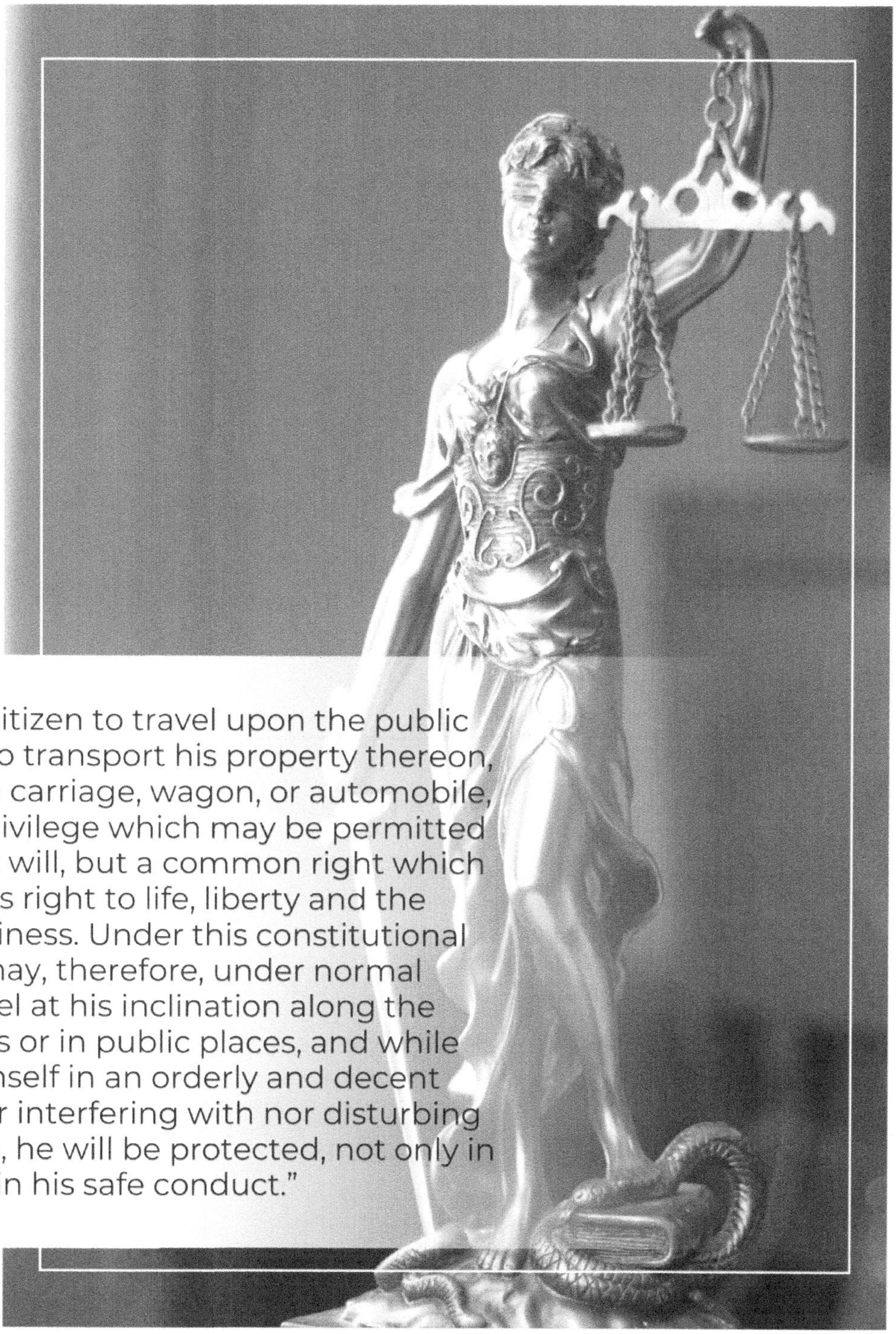

"The right of a citizen to travel upon the public highways and to transport his property thereon, by horse-drawn carriage, wagon, or automobile, is not a mere privilege which may be permitted or prohibited at will, but a common right which he has under his right to life, liberty and the pursuit of happiness. Under this constitutional guaranty one may, therefore, under normal conditions, travel at his inclination along the public highways or in public places, and while conducting himself in an orderly and decent manner, neither interfering with nor disturbing another's rights, he will be protected, not only in his person, but in his safe conduct."

U.S. SUPREME COURT

AND OTHER HIGH COURT CASES

SUPREME COURT CASES

MARBURY VS. MADISON, 5 U.S. 137 -
"The constitution of the United States is the supreme law of the land. Any in conflict is null and void of law." [emphasis added]

MIRANDA VS. ARIZONA, 384 US 436, 491 -
"Where rights secured by the Constitution are involved, there can be no rule making or legislation which would abrogate them."

MURDOCK VS PENNSYLVANIA, 319 U.S. 105 -
Can the state arbitrarily convert a secured liberty, [insert your recognized right here], into a privilege, and issue a license and fee for it? NO: "No state may convert a secured liberty into a privilege, and issue a license and fee for it."

SHUTTLESWORTH VS BIRMINGHAM, ALABAMA, 373 U.S. 262 -
If a state does attempt to convert the right into a privilege and attempts to issue a license and fee for the exercise of that privilege; can it be enforced as law? NO: "If the state does convert a right into a privilege and issue a license and charge a fee for it, you can ignore the license and fee and engage in the right with impunity."

U.S. VS BISHOP, 412 U.S. 346 -
Did you willfully and with intent violate the law? NO: "Willfulness is one of the major elements, which is required to be proven in any criminal element. You will have to prove (1) that you are the party (2) that you had a method or opportunity to do the thing, and (3) that you did so with willful intent. Willful is defined as an evil motive or intent to avoid a known duty or task under the law."

KENT VS DULLES, 357 U.S. 116, 125 -
The right to travel is a part of the "liberty" of which the citizen cannot be deprived without due process of law under the Fifth Amendment. So much is conceded by the solicitor general. In Anglo-Saxon law that right was emerging at least as early as Magna Carta. Kent v. Dulles, 357 U.S. 116, 125.

People vs Battle Traffic infractions are not a crime." People v. Battle, 50 Cal. App. step 1, Super, 123 Cal. Rptr. 636, "Traffic infractions are not a crime." People v. Battle "To this end, the Fourth Amendment requires that a seizure must be based on specific objective facts indicating that society's legitimate interests require the seizure of the particular individual, or that the seizure must be carried out pursuant to a plan embodying explicit, neutral limitations on the conduct of individual officers

HURTADO VS CALIFORNIA, 110 U.S. 516 -
The State cannot diminish rights of the people.

SELF-GOVERNING QUESTIONS?

Sovereigns own their knowledge, this builds a foundation not only for self-governing with honor but for building a foundation for responsibly comprehending what the true laws in our great nation are, otherwise we might be accused of falling asleep on our watch.

Each one of these Supreme Court Cases is worth researching.

HIGH COURT CASES

THOMPSON VS SMITH, 154 SE 579, 11 - AMERICAN JURISPRUDENCE, CONSTITUTIONAL LAW, SECTION 329, PAGE 1135 -

"The right of the Citizen to travel upon the public highways and to transport his property thereon, in the ordinary course of life and business, is a common right which he has under the right to enjoy life and liberty, to acquire and possess property, and to pursue happiness and safety. It includes the right, in so doing, to use the ordinary and usual conveyances of the day, and under the existing modes of travel, includes the right to drive a horse drawn carriage or wagon thereon or to operate an automobile thereon, for the usual and ordinary purpose of life and business."

THOMPSON VS SMITH, SUPRA.; TECHE LINES VS. DANFORTH, MISS., 12 S.2D 784., -

"... the right of the citizen to drive on a public street with freedom from police interference... is a fundamental constitutional right" -White, 97 Cal.App.3d.141, 158 Cal.Rptr. 562, 566-67 (1979) "citizens have a right to drive upon the public streets of the District of Columbia or any other city absent a constitutionally sound reason for limiting their access."

CANEISHA MILLS VS D.C. 2009, -

"The use of the automobile as a necessary adjunct to the earning of a livelihood in modern life requires us in the interest of realism to conclude that the RIGHT to use an automobile on the public highways partakes of the nature of a liberty within the meaning of the Constitutional guarantees. . ."

BERBERIAN VS LUSSIER (1958) 139 A2D 869, 872, SEE ALSO: SCHECTER VS KILLINGSWORTH, 380 P.2D 136, 140; 93 ARIZ. 273 (1963). -

"The right to operate a motor vehicle [an automobile] upon the public streets and highways is not a mere privilege. It is a right of liberty, the enjoyment of which is protected by the guarantees of the federal and state constitutions."

ADAMS VS CITY OF POCATELLO, 416 P.2D 46, 48; 91 IDAHO 99 (1966)., -

"A traveler has an equal right to employ an automobile as a means of transportation and to occupy the public highways with other vehicles in common use."

CAMPBELL VS WALKER, 78 ATL. 601, 603, 2 BOYCE (DEL.) 41, -

"The owner of an automobile has the same right as the owner of other vehicles to use the highway, ***A traveler on foot has the same right to the use of the public highways as an automobile or any other vehicle."

SIMEONE VS LINDSAY, 65 ATL. 778, 779; HANNIGAN VS WRIGHT, 63 ATL. 234, 236, -

"The RIGHT of the citizen to DRIVE on the public street with freedom from police interference, unless he is engaged in suspicious conduct associated in some manner with criminality is a FUNDAMENTAL CONSTITUTIONAL RIGHT which must be protected by the courts." People v. Horton 14 Cal. App. 3rd 667 (1971) "The right to make use of an automobile as a vehicle of travel long the highways of the state, is no longer an open question. The owners thereof have the same rights in the roads and streets as the drivers of horses or those riding a bicycle or traveling in some other vehicle."

HOUSE VS CRAMER, 112 N.W. 3; 134 IOWA 374; FARNSWORTH VS TAMPA ELECTRIC CO. 57 SO. 233, 237, 62 FLA. 166, -

"The automobile may be used with safety to others users of the highway, and in its proper use upon the highways there is an equal right with the users of other vehicles properly upon the highways. The law recognizes such right of use upon general principles.

HIGH COURT CASES

BRINKMAN VS PACHOLIKE, 84 N.E. 762, 764, 41 IND. APP. 662, 666, -
"The law does not denounce motor carriages, as such, on public ways. They have an equal right with other vehicles in common use to occupy the streets and roads. It is improper to say that the driver of the horse has rights in the roads superior to the driver of the automobile. Both have the right to use the easement."

INDIANA SPRINGS CO. VS BROWN, 165 IND. 465, 468, - U.S. SUPREME COURT SAYS NO LICENSE NECESSARY TO DRIVE AUTOMOBILE ON PUBLIC HIGHWAYS/STREETS NO LICENSE IS NECESSARY COPY AND SHARE FREELY YHVH.NAME 2 -
"A highway is a public way open and free to any one who has occasion to pass along it on foot or with any kind of vehicle." Schlesinger v. City of Atlanta, 129 S.E. 861, 867, 161 Ga. 148, 159;

HOLLAND VS SHACKELFORD, 137 S.E. 2D 298, 304, 220 GA. 104; STAVOLA V. PALMER, 73 A.2D 831, 838, 136 CONN. 670, -
"There can be no question of the right of automobile owners to occupy and use the public streets of cities, or highways in the rural districts." Liebrecht v. Crandall, 126 N.W. 69, 110 Minn. 454, 456 "The word 'automobile' connotes a pleasure vehicle designed for the transportation of persons on highways."

AMERICAN MUTUAL LIABILITY INS. CO., VS CHAPUT, 60 A.2D 118, 120; 95 NH 200 MOTOR VEHICLE: 18 USC PART 1 CHAPTER 2 SECTION 31 DEFINITIONS:"(6) MOTOR VEHICLE –
The term "motor vehicle" means every description of carriage or other contrivance propelled or drawn by mechanical power and used for commercial purposes on the highways..." 10) The term "used for commercial purposes" means the carriage of persons or property for any fare, fee, rate, charge or other consideration, or directly or indirectly in connection with any business, or other undertaking intended for profit. "A motor vehicle or automobile for hire is a motor vehicle, other than an automobile stage, used for the transportation of persons for which remuneration is received."

INTERNATIONAL MOTOR TRANSIT CO. VS SEATTLE, 251 P. 120 -
"The term 'motor vehicle' is different and broader than the word 'automobile.'"

CITY OF DAYTON VS DEBROSSE, 23 NE.2D 647, 650; 62 OHIO APP. 232 -
"Thus self-driven vehicles are classified according to the use to which they are put rather than according to the means by which they are propelled" – Ex Parte Hoffert, 148 NW 20 "

THE SUPREME COURT, IN ARTHUR VS MORGAN, 112 U.S. 495, 5 S.CT. 241, 28 L.ED. 825, -
"held that carriages were properly classified as household effects, and we see no reason that automobiles should not be similarly disposed of."

HILLHOUSE VS UNITED STATES, 152 F. 163, 164 (2ND CIR. 1907) -
"...a citizen has the right to travel upon the public highways and to transport his property thereon..."

STATE VS. JOHNSON, 243 P. 1073; CUMMINS VS HOMES, 155 P. 171; PACKARD VS BANTON, 44 S.CT. 256; HADFIELD VS LUNDIN, 98 WASH 516, WILLIS VS BUCK, 263 P. L 982; BARNEY VS BOARD OF RAILROAD COMMISSIONERS, 17 P.2D 82 -
"The use of the highways for the purpose of travel and transportation is not a mere privilege, but a common and fundamental Right of which the public and the individual cannot be rightfully deprived."

HIGH COURT CASES

CHICAGO MOTOR COACH VS CHICAGO, 169 NE 22; LIGARE VS CHICAGO, 28 NE 934; BOON VS CLARK, 214 SSW 607; 25 AM.JUR. (1ST) HIGHWAYS SECT.163 -
"the right of the Citizen to travel upon the highway and to transport his property thereon in the ordinary course of life and business... is the usual and ordinary right of the Citizen, a right common to all."

EX PARTE DICKEY, (DICKEY VS DAVIS), 85 SE 781 -
"Every Citizen has an unalienable RIGHT to make use of the public highways of the state; every Citizen has full freedom to travel from place to place in the enjoyment of life and liberty." People v. Nothaus, 147 Colo. 210. "No State government entity has the power to allow or deny passage on the highways, byways, nor waterways... transporting his vehicles and personal property for either recreation or business, but by being subject only to local regulation i.e., safety, caution, traffic lights, speed limits, etc. Travel is not a privilege requiring licensing, vehicle registration, or forced insurances."

CHICAGO COACH CO. VS CITY OF CHICAGO, 337 ILL. 200, 169 N.E. 22 -
"Traffic infractions are not a crime." People v. Battle "Persons faced with an unconstitutional licensing law which purports to require a license as a prerequisite to exercise of right... may ignore the law and engage with impunity in exercise of such right."

SHUTTLESWORTH VS BIRMINGHAM 394 U.S. 147 (1969) -
U.S. Supreme Court says No License Necessary To Drive Automobile On Public Highways/Streets No License Is Necessary Copy and Share Freely YHVH.name 3 "The word 'operator' shall not include any person who solely transports his own property and who transports no persons or property for hire or compensation."

STATUTES AT LARGE CALIFORNIA CHAPTER 412 P.83 -
"Highways are for the use of the traveling public, and all have the right to use them in a reasonable and proper manner; the use thereof is an inalienable right of every citizen." Escobedo v. State 35 C2d 870 in 8 Cal Jur 3d p.27 "RIGHT — A legal RIGHT, a constitutional RIGHT means a RIGHT protected by the law, by the constitution, but government does not create the idea of RIGHT or original RIGHTS; it acknowledges them..." Bouvier's Law Dictionary, 1914, p. 2961. "Those who have the right to do something cannot be licensed for what they already have right to do as such license would be meaningless."

CITY OF CHICAGO VS COLLINS 51 NE 907, 910 -
"A license means leave to do a thing which the licensor could prevent." Blatz Brewing Co. v. Collins, 160 P.2d 37, 39; 69 City of Chicago v Collins 51 NE 907, 910. "A license means leave to do a thing which the licensor could prevent." Blatz Brewing Co. v. Collins, 160 P.2d 37, 39; 69 Cal. A. 2d 639. "The object of a license is to confer a right or power, which does not exist without it."

PAYNE VS MASSEY (19__) 196 SW 2ND 493, 145 TEX 273 -
"The court makes it clear that a license relates to qualifications to engage in profession, business, trade or calling; thus, when merely traveling without compensation or profit, outside of business enterprise or adventure with the corporate state, no license is required of the natural individual traveling for personal business, pleasure and transportation."

WINGFIELD VS FIELDER 2D CA. 3D 213 (1972) -
"If [state] officials construe a vague statute unconstitutionally, the citizen may take them at their word, and act on the assumption that the statute is void."

HIGH COURT CASES

SHUTTLESWORTH VS BIRMINGHAM 394 U.S. 147 (1969). -
"With regard particularly to the U.S. Constitution, it is elementary that a Right secured or protected by that document cannot be overthrown or impaired by any state police authority." Donnolly vs. Union Sewer Pipe Co., 184 US 540; Lafarier vs. Grand Trunk R.R. Co., 24 A. 848; O'Neil vs. Providence Amusement Co., 108 A. 887. "The right to travel (called the right of free ingress to other states, and egress from them) is so fundamental that it appears in the Articles of Confederation, which governed our society before the Constitution."

(PAUL VS VIRGINIA). -
"[T]he right to travel freely from State to State ... is a right broadly assertable against private interference as well as governmental action. Like the right of association, it is a virtually unconditional personal right, guaranteed by the Constitution to us all."

(U.S. SUPREME COURT, SHAPRIO VS THOMPSON). -
EDGERTON, Chief Judge: "Iron curtains have no place in a free world. ...'Undoubtedly the right of locomotion, the right to remove from one place to another according to inclination, is an attribute of personal liberty, and the right, ordinarily, of free transit from or through the territory of any State is a right secured by the Constitution.'

WILLIAMS VS FEARS, 179 U.S. 270, 274, 21 S.CT. 128, 45 L.ED. 186 -
"Our nation has thrived on the principle that, outside areas of plainly harmful conduct, every American is left to shape his own life as he thinks best, do what he pleases, go where he pleases." Id., at 197.

KENT VS. DULLES SEE VESTAL, FREEDOM OF MOVEMENT, 41 IOWA L.REV. 6, 13—14 -
"The validity of restrictions on the freedom of movement of particular individuals, both substantively and procedurally, is precisely the sort of matter that is the peculiar domain of the courts." Comment, 61 Yale L.J. at page 187. "a person detained for an investigatory stop can be questioned but is "not obliged to answer, answers may not be compelled, and refusal to answer furnishes no basis for an arrest."Justice White, Hiibel "Automobiles have the right to use the highways of the State on an equal footing with other vehicles."

CUMBERLAND TELEPHONE. & TELEGRAPH CO. VS YEISER 141 KENTUCY 15 -
"Each citizen has the absolute right to choose for himself the mode of conveyance he desires, whether it be by wagon or carriage, by horse, motor or electric car, or by bicycle, or astride of a horse, subject to the sole condition that he will observe all those requirements that are known as the law of the road."

SWIFT VS CITY OF TOPEKA - 43 U.S. SUPREME COURT SAYS "NO LICENSE NECESSARY TO DRIVE AUTOMOBILE ON PUBLIC HIGHWAYS/STREETS, NO LICENSE IS NECESSARY 4 KANSAS 671, 674. THE SUPREME COURT SAID IN U.S. VS MERSKY (1960) 361 U.S. 431: -
An administrative regulation, of course, is not a "statute." A traveler on foot has the same right to use of the public highway as an automobile or any other vehicle.

CECCHI VS LINDSAY, 75 ATL. 376, 377, 1 BOYCE (DEL.) 185 -
Automotive vehicles are lawful means of conveyance and have equal rights upon the streets with horses and carriages.

HIGH COURT CASES

CHICAGO COACH CO. VS CITY OF CHICAGO, 337 ILL. 200, 205; - SEE ALSO: CHRISTY VS ELLIOT, 216 ILL. 31; WARD VS MEREDITH, 202 ILL. 66; SHINKLE VS MCCULLOUGH, 116 KY. 960; BUTLER VS CABE, 116 ARK. 26, 28-29 -
...automobiles are lawful vehicles and have equal rights on the highways with horses and carriages. Daily v. Maxwell, 133 S.W. 351, 354.

MATSON VS DAWSON, 178 N.W. 2D 588, 591 -
A farmer has the same right to the use of the highways of the state, whether on foot or in a motor vehicle, as any other citizen.

DRAFFIN VS MASSEY, 92 S.E.2D 38, 42 -
Persons may lawfully ride in automobiles, as they may lawfully ride on bicycles. Doherty v. Ayer, 83 N.E. 677, 197 Mass. 241, 246;

MOLWAY VS CITY OF CHICAGO, 88 N.E. 485, 486, 239 ILL. 486; SMILEY VS EAST ST. LOUIS RY. CO., 100 N.E. 157, 158 -
"A soldier's personal automobile is part of his 'household goods[.]'

U.S. VS BOMAR, C.A.5(TEX.), 8 F.3D 226, 235 19A WORDS AND PHRASES – PERMANENT EDITION (WEST) POCKET PART 94. -
"[I]t is a jury question whether ... an automobile ... is a motor vehicle[.]"

OTHER RIGHT TO USE AN AUTOMOBILE CASES: –

UNITED STATES V JOHNSON, 718 F.2D 1317, 1324 (5TH CIR. 1983)
EDWARDS VS. CALIFORNIA, 314 U.S. 160
TWINING VS NEW JERSEY, 211 U.S. 78
WILLIAMS VS. FEARS, 179 U.S. 270, AT 274
CRANDALL VS. NEVADA, 6 WALL. 35, AT 43-44
THE PASSENGER CASES, 7 HOWARD 287, AT 492
U.S. VS. GUEST, 383 U.S. 745, AT 757-758 (1966)
GRIFFIN VS. BRECKENRIDGE, 403 U.S. 88, AT 105-106 (1971)
CALIFANO VS. TORRES, 435 U.S. 1, AT 4, note 6
SHAPIRO VS. THOMPSON, 394 U.S. 618 (1969)
CALIFANO VS. AZNAVORIAN, 439 U.S. 170, AT 176 (1978)

Look the above citations up in American Jurisprudence. Some citations may be paraphrased.

HIGH COURT CASES

A CAR IS NOT A "MOTOR VEHICLE"

USC TITLE 18, § 31 9(6) -
Definition of "Motor Vehicle": "The term "motor vehicle" means every description of carriage or other contrivance propelled or drawn by mechanical power and used for commercial purposes on the highways in the transportation of passengers and property, or property or cargo."

USC TITLE 18, § 31(10) -
Definition of "Commercial Purposes": "The term "used for commercial purposes" means the carriage of the persons or property for any fare, fee, rate, charge or other consideration, or directly or indirectly in connection with any business, or other undertaking for profit."

So your car, SUV, or motorcycle is only a "commercial vehicle" if you are getting paid to "drive" it. If you are only using it to travel around to go to work, school, groceries, or any other private reason then it IS NOT A "MOTOR VEHICLE".

Here is the dilemma, when the government started requiring the commercial vehicles to be registered and licensed it made that a regulable activity for that purpose. They made everyone else believe it was the same for the general public. The police, you, and all your friends are taught that you are always 'operating' a 'motor vehicle' which are both commercial regulable activities.

May the state change the definition of a word or term (MOTOR VEHICLE) from the original meaning (USC Title 18, § 31 (6) to another definition to fit their own needs? NO:

CRAIG VS MISSOURI, U S 29, 410 -
The state cannot change the meaning of "motor vehicle" and "driver" to fit their own needs: "Is the proposition to be maintained, that the constitution meant to prohibit names and not things? That a very important act, big with great and ruinous mischief which is expressly forbidden by words most appropriate for its description; may be performed by the substitution of a name? That the constitution, in one of its most important provisions, may be openly evaded by giving a new name to an old thing? We cannot think so." [...The State] cannot change the name of a thing to avoid the mandates of the Constitution.]"

What the United States Supreme Court, the highest court in the land, says here is that the state cannot change the meaning of "person traveling" to "driver", and they cannot change the name or term of "private car," "pickup" or "motorcycle" to "Motor Vehicle". C

HIGH COURT CASES

TRAVELING VS DRIVING

SHAPIRO VS THOMPSON 394 US 618 -
"All citizens must be free to travel throughout the United States uninhibited by statutes, rules, and regulations..."

THOMPSON VS SMITH, 155 VA 367 -
"The RIGHT of the citizen TO TRAVEL UPON THE PUBLIC HIGHWAYS and to transport his property thereon, either by horse-drawn carriage OR BY AUTOMOBILE, IS NOT A MERE PRIVILEGE which the city may prohibit or permit at will, BUT IS A COMMON RIGHT."

CHICAGO MOTOR COACH VS CHICAGO, 169 NE 221 CHICAGO, 337 ILL. 200, 169 NE 22, 66 ALR 834. LIGARE VS CHICAGO , 139 ILL. 46, 28 NE 934. BOONE VS CLARK JUR (1ST) HIGHWAYS, SEC. 163. , 214 SW 607; 25 A M -
"The use of the highway for the purpose of travel and transportation is not a mere privilege, but a common fundamental right of which the public and individuals cannot rightfully be deprived."

SHUTTLESWORTH VS BIRMINGHAM, ALABAMA, 373 US 262 -
"If the state does convert your right into a privilege and issue a license and charge a fee for it, you can ignore the license and fee and engage in the right with impunity."

PRACTICING LAW WITHOUT A LICENSE

NAACP VS BUTTON THE COURT HELD THAT THE ACTIVITIES OF THE NAACP AMOUNTED TO - "modes of expression and association protected by the First and Fourteenth Amendments which Virginia may not prohibit." NAACP-initiated litigation was "a form of political expression" and not "a technique of resolving private differences,"

SCHWARE VS BOARD OF EXAMINERS 353 U.S. 232 (1957) - There is no such thing as an Attorney License to practice law. The UNITED STATES SUPREME COURT held a long time ago that 'The practice of Law CAN NOT be licensed by any state/State.'

"A State cannot exclude a person from the practice of law or from any other occupation in a manner or for reasons that contravene the Due Process or Equal Protection [353 U.S. 232, 239] Clause of the Fourteenth Amendment. Further, as a CERTIFICATE IS NOT A LICENSE then it also gives no power to anyone to practice Law AS AN OCCUPATION, nor to DO BUSINESS AS A LAW FIRM."

SIMS VS AHRENS, 271 S.W. 720 (1925) - "The practice of Law is an occupation of common right." Further, The state bar association is not a government entity. The state bar association...is a "PROFESSIONAL ASSOCIATION" and their "STATE BAR" CARD IS NOT A LICENSE either. All that card is – is a "UNION DUES CARD" like the Actors Union, Painters Union, Electricians union etc.

- Hosea 4:6 -

"My people are destroyed for lack of knowledge".

DEFINITIONS

AND TERMS

AUTOMOBILE vs MOTOR VEHICLE

There is a clear distinction between an automobile and a motor vehicle. An automobile has been defined as:

AMERICAN MUTUAL LIABILITY INS. CO., VS. CHAPUT, 60 A.2D 118, 120; 95 NH 200
"The word 'automobile' connotes a pleasure vehicle designed for the transportation of persons on highways."

While the distinction is made clear between the two as the courts have stated:

INTERNATIONAL MOTOR TRANSIT CO. VS. SEATTLE, 251 P. 120
"A motor vehicle or automobile for hire is a motor vehicle, other than an automobile stage, used for the transportation of persons for which remuneration is received."

CITY OF DAYTON VS. DEBROSSE, 23 NE.2D 647, 650; 62 OHIO APP. 232
The term 'motor vehicle' is different and broader than the word 'automobile'."

The distinction is made very clear in - Title 18 USC 31:

"MOTOR VEHICLE"
means every description or other contrivance propelled or drawn by mechanical power and used for commercial purposes on the highways in the transportation of passengers, or passengers and property.

"USED FOR COMMERCIAL PURPOSES"
means the carriage of persons or property for any fare, fee, rate, charge, or other considerations, or directly or indirectly in connection with any business, or other undertaking intended for profit.

An automobile is used for private purposes, while a motor vehicle is considered a machine that may be used on highways for trade, commerce, or hire.

MOTOR VEHICLE

A visor card guide for state and local law enforcement officials outlining the types of commercial motor vehicles and their configurations

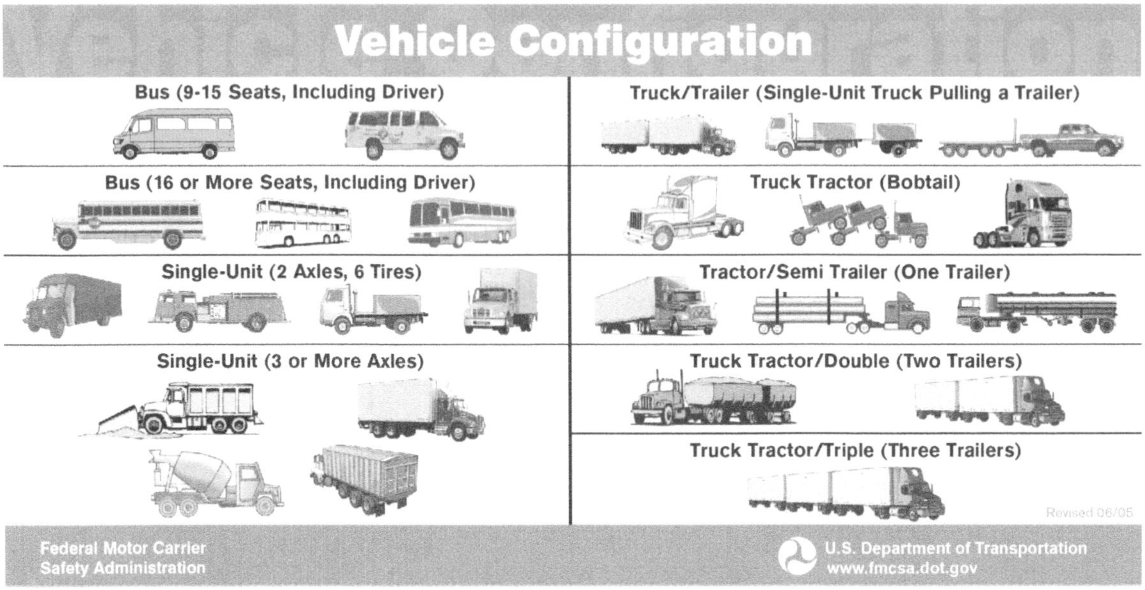

Vehicle Configuration: Provides information about the general size and design of the motor vehicle. This element is important to evaluate the types of motor vehicles that have the most crashes and the effectiveness of various safety countermeasures.

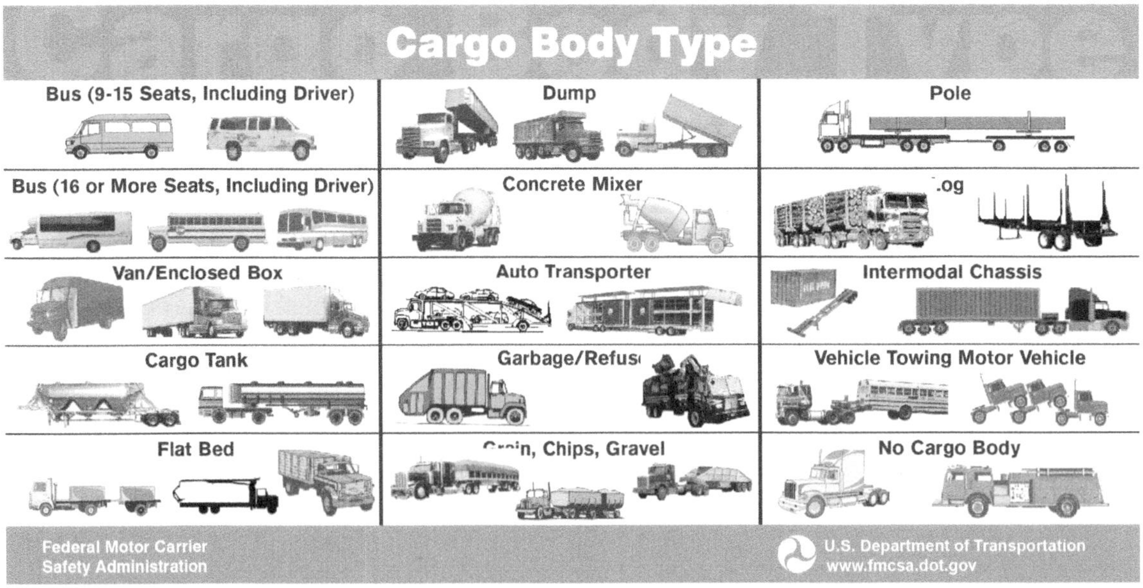

Cargo Body Type: A description of the vehicle's primary cargo-carrying capability, it provides additional information about the motor vehicle. The information it provides can be important in helping FMCSA make decisions on regulatory strategies for different types of motor vehicles.

DUE PROCESS

PAGE 1

SIMON VS. CRAFT, 182 US 427
"The essential elements of due process of law are ... Notice and The Opportunity to defend."

Yet, not one individual has been given notice of the loss of his/her Right, let alone before signing the license (contract). Nor was the Citizen given any opportunity to defend against the loss of his/her right to travel, by automobile, on the highways, in the ordinary course of life and business. This amounts to an arbitrary deprivation of Liberty.

BARBOUR VS. CONNOLLY, 113 US 27, 31; YICK WO VS. HOPKINS, 118 US 356
"There should be no arbitrary deprivation of Life or Liberty ..."

and ...

KENT VS. DULLES, 357 US 116 (1958)
"The right to travel is part of the Liberty of which a citizen cannot deprived without due process of law under the Fifth Amendment. This Right was emerging as early as the Magna Carta."

The focal point of this question of police power and due process must balance upon the point of making the public highways a safe place for the public to travel. If a man travels in a manner that creates actual damage, an action would lie (civilly) for recovery of damages. The state could then also proceed against the individual to deprive him of his Right to use the public highways, for cause. This process would fulfill the due process requirements of the Fifth Amendment while at the same time insuring that Rights guaranteed by the U.S. Constitution and the state constitutions would be protected.

But unless or until harm or damage (a crime) is committed, there is no cause for interference in the private affairs or actions of a Citizen.

One of the most famous and perhaps the most quoted definitions of due process of law is that of Daniel Webster in his Dartmouth College Case (4 Wheat 518), in which he declared that by due process is meant:

SEE ALSO STATE VS. STRASBURG, 110 P. 1020; DENNIS VS. MOSES, 52 P. 333
"a law which hears before it condemns, which proceeds upon inquiry, and renders judgment only after trial."

Somewhat similar is the statement that is a rule as old as the law that:

"no one shall be personally bound (restricted) until he has had his day in court,"

by which is meant, until he has been duly cited to appear and has been afforded an opportunity to be heard. Judgment without such citation and opportunity lacks all the attributes of a judicial determination; it is judicial usurpation and it is oppressive and can never be upheld where it is fairly administered. (12 Am.Jur. [1st] Const. Law, Sect. 573, Pg. 269)

NOTE: This sounds like the process used to deprive one of the "privilege" of operating a motor vehicle "for hire." It should be kept in mind, however, that we are discussing the arbitrary deprivation of the Right to use the road that all citizens have "in common."

The futility of the state's position can be most easily observed in the 1959 Washington Attorney General's opinion on a similar issue:

"The distinction between the Right of the Citizen to use the public highways for private, rather than commercial purposes is recognized ..."

and ...

WASHINGTON A.G.O. 59-60 NO. 88, PG. 11

"Under its power to regulate private uses of our highways, our legislature has required that motor vehicle operators be licensed (I.C. 49-307). Undoubtedly, the primary purpose of this requirement is to insure, as far as possible, that all motor vehicle operators will be competent and qualified, thereby reducing the potential hazard or risk of harm, to which other users of the highways might otherwise be subject. But once having complied with this regulatory provision, by obtaining the required license, a motorist enjoys the privilege of traveling freely upon the highways ..."

This alarming opinion appears to be saying that every person using an automobile as a matter of Right, must give up the Right and convert the Right into a privilege. This is accomplished under the guise of regulation. This statement is indicative of the insensitivity, even the ignorance, of the government to the limits placed upon governments by and through the several constitutions.

This legal theory may have been able to stand in 1959; however, as of 1966, in the United States Supreme Court decision in Miranda, even this weak defense of the state's actions must fall.

MIRANDA VS. ARIZONA, 384 US 436, 491

"Where rights secured by the Constitution are involved, there can be no rulemaking or legislation which would abrogate them."

Thus the legislature does not have the power to abrogate the Citizen's Right to travel upon the public roads, by passing legislation forcing the citizen to waive his Right and convert that Right into a privilege. Furthermore, we have previously established that this "privilege" has been defined as applying only to those who are "conducting business in the streets" or "operating for-hire vehicles."

The legislature has attempted (by legislative fiat) to deprive the Citizen of his Right to use the roads in the ordinary course of life and business, without affording the Citizen the safeguard of "due process of law." This has been accomplished under supposed powers of regulation.

CONVERSION OF A RIGHT TO A CRIME

As previously demonstrated, the Citizen has the Right to travel and to transport his property upon the public highways in the ordinary course of life and business. However, if one exercises this Right to travel (without first giving up the Right and converting that Right into a privilege) the Citizen is by statute, guilty of a crime. This amounts to converting the exercise of a Constitutional Right into a crime.

HURTADO VS. CALIFORNIA, 110 US 516 - RECALL THE MILLER VS. U.S. AND SNERER VS. CULLEN QUOTES FROM PG. 5, AND:
"The state cannot diminish Rights of the people."

and ...

MIRANDA, SUPRA.
"Where rights secured by the Constitution are involved, there can be no rulemaking or legislation which would abrogate them."

Indeed, the very purpose for creating the state under the limitations of the constitution was to protect the rights of the people from intrusion, particularly by the forces of government.

So we can see that any attempt by the legislature to make the act of using the public highways as a matter of Right into a crime, is void upon its face.

Any person who claims his Right to travel upon the highways, and so exercises that Right, cannot be tried for a crime of doing so. And yet, this Freeman stands before this court today to answer charges for the "crime" of exercising his Right to Liberty.

As we have already shown, the term "drive" can only apply to those who are employed in the business of transportation for hire. It has been shown that freedom includes the Citizen's Right to use the public highways in the ordinary course of life and business without license or regulation by the police powers of the state.

LICENSE

It seems only proper to define the word "license," as the definition of this word will be extremely important in understanding the statutes as they are properly applied:

PEOPLE VS. HENDERSON, 218 NW.2D 2, 4
"The permission, by competent authority to do an act which without permission, would be illegal, a trespass, or a tort."

WESTERN ELECTRIC CO. VS. PACENT REPRODUCER CORP., 42 F.2D 116, 118
"Leave to do a thing which licensor could prevent."

In order for these two definitions to apply in this case, the state would have to take up the position that the exercise of a Constitutional Right to use the public roads in the ordinary course of life and business is illegal, a trespass, or a tort, which the state could then regulate or prevent.

This position, however, would raise magnitudinous Constitutional questions as this position would be diametrically opposed to fundamental Constitutional Law. (See "Conversion of a Right to a Crime," infra.)

In the instant case, the proper definition of a "license" is:

ROSENBLATT VS. CALIFORNIA STATE BOARD OF PHARMACY, 158 P.2D 199, 203
"a permit, granted by an appropriate governmental body, generally for consideration, to a person, firm, or corporation, to pursue some occupation or to carry on some business which is subject to regulation under the police power."

This definition would fall more in line with the "privilege" of carrying on business on the streets.
Most people tend to think that "licensing" is imposed by the state for the purpose of raising revenue, yet there may well be more subtle reasons contemplated; for when one seeks permission from someone to do something he invokes the jurisdiction of the "licensor" which, in this case, is the state. In essence, the licensee may well be seeking to be regulated by the "licensor."

STATE VS. JACKSON, 60 WISC.2D 700; 211 NW.2D 480, 487
"A license fee is a charge made primarily for regulation, with the fee to cover costs and expenses of supervision or regulation."

The fee is the price; the regulation or control of the licensee is the real aim of the legislation.

POLICE POWER

PAGE 1

The confusion of the police power with the power of taxation usually arises in cases where the police power has affixed a penalty to a certain act, or where it requires licenses to be obtained and a certain sum to be paid for certain occupations. The power used in the instant case cannot, however, be the power of taxation since an attempt to levy a tax upon a Right would be open to Constitutional objection. (See "taxing power," infra.)

EACH LAW RELATING TO THE USE OF POLICE POWER MUST ASK THREE QUESTIONS:

1. Is there threatened danger?
2. Does a regulation involve a Constitutional Right?
3. Is this regulation reasonable?

PEOPLE VS. SMITH, 108 AM.ST.REP. 715; BOVIER'S LAW DICTIONARY, 1914 ED., UNDER "POLICE POWER"

When applying these three questions to the statute in question, some very important issues emerge.

1. First, "is there a threatened danger" in the individual using his automobile on the public highways, in the ordinary course of life and business?

The answer is No! There is nothing inherently dangerous in the use of an automobile when it is carefully managed. Their guidance, speed, and noise are subject to quick and easy control, under a competent and considerate manager, it is as harmless on the road as a horse and buggy.

It is the manner of managing the automobile, and that alone, which threatens the safety of the public. The ability to stop quickly and to respond quickly to guidance would seem to make the automobile one of the least dangerous conveyances. (See Yale Law Journal, December 1905.)

COHENS VS. MEADOW, 89 SE 876; BLAIR VS. BROADMORE, 93 SE 532
"The automobile is not inherently dangerous."

To deprive all persons of the Right to use the road in the ordinary course of life and business, because one might, in the future, become dangerous, would be a deprivation not only of the Right to travel, but also the Right to due process. (See "Due Process," infra.)

2. Next: does the regulation involve a Constitutional Right?

This question has already been addressed and answered in this brief, and need not be reinforced other than to remind this Court that this Citizen does have the Right to travel upon the public highway by automobile in the ordinary course of life and business. It can therefore be concluded that this regulation does involve a Constitutional Right.

3. The third question above is the most important in this case. "Is this regulation reasonable?"

The answer is No! It will be shown later in "Regulation," infra., that this licensing statute is oppressive and could be effectively administered by less oppressive means.

Although the Fourteenth Amendment does not interfere with the proper exercise of the police power, in accordance with the general principle that the power must be exercised so as not to invade unreasonably the rights guaranteed by the United States Constitution, it is established beyond question that every state power, including the police power, is limited by the Fourteenth Amendment (and others) and by the inhibitions there imposed.

Moreover, the ultimate test of the propriety of police power regulations must be found in the Fourteenth Amendment, since it operates to limit the field of the police power to the extent of preventing the enforcement of statutes in denial of Rights that the Amendment protects. (See Parks vs. State, 64 NE 682.)

<u>CONNOLLY VS. UNION SEWER PIPE CO., 184 US 540; LAFARIER VS. GRAND TRUNK R.R. CO., 24 A. 848; O'NEIL VS. PROVIDENCE AMUSEMENT CO., 108 A. 887</u>
"With regard particularly to the U.S. Constitution, it is elementary that a Right secured or protected by that document cannot be overthrown or impaired by any state police authority."

<u>BACAHANAN VS. WANLEY, 245 US 60; PANHANDLE EASTERN PIPELINE CO. VS. STATE HIGHWAY COMMISSION, 294 US 613</u>
"The police power of the state must be exercised in subordination to the provisions of the U.S. Constitution."

<u>TICHE VS. OSBORNE, 131 A. 60</u>
"It is well settled that the Constitutional Rights protected from invasion by the police power, include Rights safeguarded both by express and implied prohibitions in the Constitutions."

<u>MEHLOS VS. MILWAUKEE, 146 NW 882</u>
"As a rule, fundamental limitations of regulations under the police power are found in the spirit of the Constitutions, not in the letter, although they are just as efficient as if expressed in the clearest language."

As it applies in the instant case, the language of the Fifth Amendment is clear:

"No person shall be ... deprived of Life, Liberty, or Property without due process of law."

As has been shown, the courts at all levels have firmly established an absolute Right to travel.

In the instant case, the state, by applying commercial statutes to all entities, natural and artificial persons alike, has deprived this free and natural person of the Right of Liberty, without cause and without due process of law.

REGULATIONS

PAGE 1

25 AM.JUR. (1ST) HIGHWAYS, SECT. 260

"In addition to the requirement that regulations governing the use of the highways must not be violative of constitutional guarantees, the prime essentials of such regulation are reasonableness, impartiality, and definiteness or certainty."

and ...

DAVIS VS. MASSACHUSETTS, 167 US 43; PACHARD VS. BANTON, SUPRA.

"Moreover, a distinction must be observed between the regulation of an activity which may be engaged in as a matter of right and one carried on by government sufferance of permission."

One can say for certain that these regulations are impartial since they are being applied to all, even though they are clearly beyond the limits of the legislative powers. However, we must consider whether such regulations are reasonable and non-violative of constitutional guarantees.

First, let us consider the reasonableness of this statute requiring all persons to be licensed (presuming that we are applying this statute to all persons using the public roads). In determining the reasonableness of the statute we need only ask two questions:

1. Does the statute accomplish its stated goal? The answer is No!

The attempted explanation for this regulation "to insure the safety of the public by insuring, as much as possible, that all are competent and qualified."

However, one can keep his license without retesting, from the time he/she is first licensed until the day he/she dies, without regard to the competency of the person, by merely renewing said license before it expires. It is therefore possible to completely skirt the goal of this attempted regulation, thus proving that this regulation does not accomplish its goal.

Furthermore, by testing and licensing, the state gives the appearance of underwriting the competence of the licensees, and could therefore be held liable for failures, accidents, etc. caused by licensees.

2. Is the statute reasonable? The answer is No!

This statute cannot be determined to be reasonable since it requires to the Citizen to give up his or her natural Right to travel unrestricted in order to accept the privilege. The purported goal of this statute could be met by much less oppressive regulations, i.e., competency tests and certificates of competency before using an automobile upon the public roads. (This is exactly the situation in the aviation sector.)

But isn't this what we have now? The answer is No! The real purpose of this license is much more insidious. When one signs the license, he/she gives up his/her Constitutional Right to travel in order to accept and exercise a privilege. After signing the license, a quasi-contract, the Citizen has to give the state his/her consent to be prosecuted for constructive crimes and quasi-criminal actions where there is no harm done and no damaged property.

PAGE 2

"These prosecutions take place without affording the Citizen of their Constitutional Rights and guarantees, such as the Right to a trial by jury of twelve persons and the Right to counsel, as well as, the normal safeguards such as proof of intent and a corpus dilecti and a grand jury indictment. These unconstitutional prosecutions take place because the Citizen is exercising a privilege and has given his/her "implied consent" to legislative enactments designed to control interstate commerce, a regulatable enterprise under the police power of the state.

We must now conclude that the Citizen is forced to give up Constitutional guarantees of "Right" in order to exercise his state "privilege" to travel upon the public highways in the ordinary course of life and business.

SURRENDER OF RIGHTS

"A Citizen cannot be forced to give up his/her Rights in the name of regulation.

RILEY VS. LAESON, 142 SO. 619; STEPHENSON VS. BINFORD, SUPRA.
"... the only limitations found restricting the right of the state to condition the use of the public highways as a means of vehicular transportation for compensation are (1) that the state must not exact of those it permits to use the highways for hauling for gain that they surrender any of their inherent U.S. Constitutional Rights as a condition precedent to obtaining permission for such use ..."

If one cannot be placed in a position of being forced to surrender Rights in order to exercise a privilege, how much more must this maxim of law, then, apply when one is simply exercising (putting into use) a Right?

HOKE VS. HENDERSON, 15 NC 15
"To be that statute which would deprive a Citizen of the rights of person or property,
without a regular trial, according to the course and usage of the common law,
would not be the law of the land."

and ...

SIMONS VS. UNITED STATES, 390 US 389
"We find it intolerable that one Constitutional Right should have to be surrendered
in order to assert another."

Since the state requires that one give up Rights in order to exercise the privilege of driving, the regulation cannot stand under the police power, due process, or regulation, but must be exposed as a statute which is oppressive and one which has been misapplied to deprive the Citizen of Rights guaranteed by the United States Constitution and the state constitutions.

TRAFFIC

Having defined the terms "automobile," "motor vehicle," "traveler," "driver," and "operator," the next term to define is "traffic":

NORTHERN PACIFIC R.R. CO. VS. SCHOENFELDT, 213 P. 26
"... Traffic thereon is to some extent destructive, therefore, the prevention of unnecessary duplication of auto transportation service will lengthen the life of the highways or reduce the cost of maintenance, the revenue derived by the state ... will also tend toward the public welfare by producing at the expense of those operating for private gain, some small part of the cost of repairing the wear ..."

Note: In the above, Justice Tolman expounded upon the key of raising revenue by taxing the "privilege" to use the public roads "at the expense of those operating for gain."

In this case, the word "traffic" is used in conjunction with the unnecessary Auto Transportation Service, or in other words, "vehicles for hire." The word "traffic" is another word which is to be strictly construed to the conducting of business.

BOVIER'S LAW DICTIONARY, 1914 ED., PG. 3307
"Traffic Commerce, trade, sale or exchange of merchandise, bills, money, or the like. The passing of goods and commodities from one person to another for an equivalent in goods or money ..."

Here again, notice that this definition refers to one "conducting business." No mention is made of one who is traveling in his automobile. This definition is of one who is engaged in the passing of a commodity or goods in exchange for money, i.e .., vehicles for hire.

Furthermore, the word "traffic" and "travel" must have different meanings which the courts recognize. The difference is recognized in Ex Parte Dickey, supra:

"...in addition to this, cabs, hackney coaches, omnibuses, taxicabs, and hacks, when unnecessarily numerous, interfere with the ordinary traffic and travel and obstruct them."

The court, by using both terms, signified its recognition of a distinction between the two. But, what was the distinction? We have already defined both terms, but to clear up any doubt:

ALLEN VS. CITY OF BELLINGHAM, 163 P. 18
"The word `traffic' is manifestly used here in secondary sense, and has reference to the business of transportation rather than to its primary meaning of interchange of commodities."

Here the Supreme Court of the State of Washington has defined the word "traffic" (in either its primary or secondary sense) in reference to business, and not to mere travel! So it is clear that the term "traffic" is business related and therefore, it is a "privilege." The net result being that "traffic" is brought under the (police) power of the legislature. The term has no application to one who is not using the roads as a place of business.

TRAVELER VS DRIVER/OPERATOR

The term "travel" is a significant term and is defined as:

25 AM.JUR. (1ST) HIGHWAYS, SECT.427, PG. 717
"The term `travel' and `traveler' are usually construed in their broad and general sense ... so as to include all those who rightfully use the highways viatically (when being reimbursed for expenses) and who have occasion to pass over them for the purpose of business, convenience, or pleasure."

LOCKET VS. STATE, 47 ALA. 45; BOVIER'S LAW DICTIONARY, 1914 ED., PG. 3309

- "Traveler - One who passes from place to place, whether for pleasure, instruction, business, or health."
- "Travel - To journey or to pass through or over; as a country district, road, etc. To go from one place to another, whether on foot, or horseback, or in any conveyance as a train, an automobile, carriage, ship, or aircraft; Make a journey." Century Dictionary, Pg. 2034

Therefore, the term "travel" or "traveler" refers to one who uses a conveyance to go from one place to another and included all those who use the highways as a matter of Right.

Notice that in all these definitions, the phrase "for hire" never occurs. This term "travel" or "traveler" implies, by definition, one who uses the road as a means to move from one place to another.

Therefore, one who uses the road in the ordinary course of life and business for the purpose of travel and transportation is a traveler.

The term "driver" in contradistinction to "traveler," is defined as:

BOVIER'S LAW DICTIONARY, 1914 ED., PG. 940
"Driver -- One employed in conducting a coach, carriage, wagon, or other vehicles..."

Notice that this definition includes one who is "employed" in conducting a vehicle. It should be self-evident that this individual could not be "traveling" on a journey but is using the road as a place of business.

Today we assume that a "traveler" is a "driver," and a "driver" is an "operator." However, this is not the case.

NEWBILL VS. UNION INDEMNITY CO., 60 SE.2D 658
"It will be observed from the language of the ordinance that a distinction is to be drawn between the terms `operator' and `driver'; the `operator' of the service car being the person who is licensed to have the car on the streets in the business of carrying passengers for hire; while the `driver' is the one who actually drives the car. However, in the actual prosecution of business, it was possible for the same person to be both `operator' and `driver.'"

- William Pen -

"Men must be Governed by God or they will be Governed by Tyrants"

HIGHEST FORM OF LAW

THE BIBLE

PROPERTY 18 U.S. CODE 247

18 USC ss247- Damage to religious property; obstruction of persons in the free exercise of religious beliefs

(a)Whoever, in any of the circumstances referred to in subsection (b) of this section—
(1) intentionally defaces, damages, or destroys any religious real property, because of the religious character of that property, or attempts to do so; or
(2) intentionally obstructs, by force or threat of force, including by threat of force against religious real property, any person in the enjoyment of that person's free exercise of religious beliefs, or attempts to do so; shall be punished as provided in subsection (d).
(b) The circumstances referred to in subsection (a) are that the offense is in or affects interstate or foreign commerce.
(d)
(1) if death results from acts committed in violation of this section...imprisonment for any term of years, or for life, or both, or may be sentenced to death;
(2) if bodily injury results to any person, a fine under this title or imprisonment for not more than 40 years, or both;

Exodus 34:14.15 "The Lord is known for devotion and He says be careful not to make a covenant with the inhabitants of the land...

1 Thessalonians 4:4 *"...that each of you know how to acquire control of his own vessel.."*

Proverbs 6:1-7 *"My son, if you have put up security for your neighbor, you have been ensnared... caught by the words of your mouth, do this, my son, and free yourself, for you have fallen into the hands of your neighbor... Do not allow your eyes to sleep, nor your eyelids to slumber. Free yourself like a gazelle from the hunter's hand, like a bird from the hand of the Fowler."*

Proverbs 1:10 *"My son, if sinners try to seducé you, do not consent."*

Proverbs 14:12 *"There exists a way that is upright before a man, but the ways of death are at the end of it."*

Proverbs 1:18-19 *"Consequently, they themselves lie in ambush for the very blood of these; they lie in concealment for their souls. Thus are the paths of everyone making an unjust profit. It takes away the very soul of its owner.?*

Matthew 6:33 *"Keep on, then, seeking first the Kingdom and His righteousness..."*

1 Corinthians 6:19-20 *"Do you not know that the body is the temple of the Holy Spirit within you which you have received from The Lord? Also, you do not belong to yourselves, for you were bought for a price. By all means, glorify Him in the body."*

Ephesians 4:23 *"Continue to be made new in your dominant mental attitude."*

Revelation 18:4 *"Get out of her, my people, if you do not want to share with her in her sins, and if you do not want to receive part of her plagues."*

Acts 5:29 *"...We must obey The Lord rather than man."*

Joshua 1:9 *"Have I not commanded you? Be courageous and strong. Do not be struck with terror or fear, for The Lord your God is with you wherever you go."*

---

https://www.law.cornell.edu/uscode/text/18/247

PUBLIC LAW 97-280

PUBLIC LAW 97-280—OCT. 4, 1982 96 STAT. 1211

Public Law 97-280
97th Congress

JOINT RESOLUTION

Authorizing and requesting the President to proclaim 1983 as the "Year of the Bible".

Whereas the Bible, the Word of God, has made a unique contribution in shaping the United States as a distinctive and blessed nation and people;

Whereas deeply held religious convictions springing from the Holy Scriptures led to the early settlement of our Nation;

Whereas Biblical teachings inspired concepts of civil government that are contained in our Declaration of Independence and the Constitution of the United States;

Whereas many of our great national leaders—among them Presidents Washington, Jackson, Lincoln, and Wilson—paid tribute to the surpassing influence of the Bible in our country's development, as in the words of President Jackson that the Bible is "the rock on which our Republic rests";

Whereas the history of our Nation clearly illustrates the value of voluntarily applying the teachings of the Scriptures in the lives of individuals, families, and societies;

Whereas this Nation now faces great challenges that will test this Nation as it has never been tested before; and

Whereas that renewing our knowledge of and faith in God through Holy Scripture can strengthen us as a nation and a people: Now, therefore, be it Resolved by the Senate and House of Representatives of the United States of America in Congress assembled, That the President is authorized and requested to designate 1983 as a national "Year of the Bible" in recognition of both the formative influence the Bible has been for our Nation and our national need to study and apply the teachings of the Holy Scriptures.

https://www.congress.gov/97/statute/STATUTE-96/STATUTE-96-Pg1211.pdf

- Supreme Court of Iowa -

"The right to make use of an automobile as a vehile of travel along the highway of the state, is no longer an open question. The owners thereof have the same rights in the roads and streets as the drivers of horses or those riding a bicycle."

ADDITIONAL
RESOURCES

TRUSTED SOURCES

- AMERICAS-ASSEMBLY.COM
- THETEXASREPUBLIC.COM
- AMERICANSTATES.US

WEBSITES

- HTTP://WWW.RULEOFLAWRADIO.COM/
- HTTPS://NATIONALLIBERTYALLIANCE.ORG/
- HTTPS://INCORPORATED.ZONE/UNDER-DURESS/
- HTTPS://LAWFULPATH.COM/REF/DLBRIEF.SHTML
- HTTPS://WWW.USLAWBOOKS.COM/TRAVEL/TRAVELCITES.HTM
- HTTPS://WWW.CONSTITUTIONALLAWGROUP.US/TRAFFIC-LAW/
- HTTPS://WWW.SOVEREIGNTYINTERNATIONAL.FYI/FREEFILES.SHTML
- HTTP://WWW.PAULSTRAMER.NET/2013/10/US-SUPREME-COURT-SAYS-NO-LICENSE.HTML
- HTTPS://CENTRAL-BAILBONDS.COM/U-S-SUPREME-COURT-SAYS-NO-LICENSE-NECESSARY-TO-DRIVE-AUTOMOBILE-ON-PUBLIC-HIGHWAYSSTREETS/
- HTTPS://WWW.LINKEDIN.COM/PULSE/US-SUPREME-COURT-SAYS-LICENSE-NECESSARY-DRIVE-PUBLIC-PAUL-LEBRETON
- HTTPS://WWW.SOVEREIGNTYINTERNATIONAL.FYI/FREEFILES/TRAFFIC_TICKET_MANUAL_VOL1.PDF
- HTTPS://WWW.SOVEREIGNTYINTERNATIONAL.FYI/FREEFILES/TRAFFIC_TICKET_MANUAL_VOL_2.PDF
- HTTPS://WWW.SOVEREIGNTYINTERNATIONAL.FYI/FREEFILES/TRAFFIC_TICKET_MANUAL_VOL_3.PDF

BOOKS

COMMON LAW HANDBOOK
FOR JUROR'S, SHERIFF'S,
BAILIFF'S, AND JUSTICE'S
Justice and judgment are the habitation of thy throne mercy and truth shall go before thy face. - Psa. 89:14
WE THE PEOPLE
"Governments are instituted among Men, deriving their Just powers from the consent of the governed"

Happy is the man that findeth wisdom, and the man that getteth understanding. - Pro. 3:13
WE THE PEOPLE

THE UCC CONNECTION
HOW TO FREE YOUSELF
FROM LEGAL TYRANNY
Happy is the man that findeth wisdom, and the man that getteth understanding. - Pro. 3:13
WE THE PEOPLE
"Governments are instituted among Men, deriving their Just powers from the consent of the governed"

THE
CONSTITUTION
of the
UNITED STATES
of AMERICA
The Declaration of Independence,
Articles of Confederation,
The Bill of Rights &
Amendments XI- XXVII

SOURCE LIST

- U.S. CONSTITUTION - FIFTH AMENDMENT | RESOURCES | CONSTITUTION ANNOTATED | CONGRESS.GOV | LIBRARY OF CONGRESS. (1791). ..GOV. HTTPS://CONSTITUTION.CONGRESS.GOV/CONSTITUTION/AMENDMENT-5/#AMENDMENT-5
- § 1–308. PERFORMANCE OR ACCEPTANCE UNDER RESERVATION OF RIGHTS. (1952). LII / LEGAL INFORMATION INSTITUTE. HTTPS://WWW.LAW.CORNELL.EDU/UCC/1/1-308
- SEC. 521.001 - (3) "DRIVER'S LICENSE." (2021). STATUTES.CAPITOL.TEXAS. HTTPS://STATUTES.CAPITOL.TEXAS.GOV/DOCS/TN/HTM/TN.521.HTM
- TRANSPORTATION CODE CHAPTER 701. COUNTY TRAFFIC OFFICERS. (N.D.). HTTPS://STATUTES.CAPITOL.TEXAS.GOV/DOCS/TN/HTM/TN.701.HTM.
- 18 U.S. CODE § 241 - CONSPIRACY AGAINST RIGHTS. (N.D.). LII / LEGAL INFORMATION INSTITUTE. HTTPS://WWW.LAW.CORNELL.EDU/USCODE/TEXT/18/241
- 18 U.S. CODE § 242 - DEPRIVATION OF RIGHTS UNDER COLOR OF LAW. (N.D.). LII / LEGAL INFORMATION INSTITUTE. HTTPS://WWW.LAW.CORNELL.EDU/USCODE/TEXT/18/242

NOTES

NOTES

NOTES

NOTES

NOTES

NOTES

NOTES

NOTES

NOTES

NOTES

NOTES

Made in the USA
Middletown, DE
05 November 2026

36544882R10044